THE WHEELING YEAR

THE WHEELING YEAR

A Poet's Field Book | TED KOOSER

UNIVERSITY OF NEBRASKA PRESS | LINCOLN & LONDON

Acknowledgments for the use of
copyrighted material appear on
page 83, which constitutes an exten-
sion of the copyright page.

Publication of this volume was
assisted by the Friends of the
University of Nebraska Press.

Library of Congress
Cataloging-in-Publication Data

Kooser, Ted.
The wheeling year: a poet's field
book / Ted Kooser.
pages cm
Summary: "A short, accessible set
of prose observations about nature,
place, and time, arranged (like Local
Wonders) according to the calendar
year"—Provided by publisher.
ISBN 978-0-8032-4970-7 (hardback:
alk. paper)
ISBN 978-0-8032-5674-3 (epub)
ISBN 978-0-8032-5675-0 (mobi)
ISBN 978-0-8032-5673-6 (pdf)
I. Title.
PS3561.O6W49 2014
811'.6—dc23
2014007299

Set in Minion Pro by L. Auten.
Designed by A. Shahan.

One day tells its tale to another

PSALM 19

PREFACE

I've always been covetous of my friend Keith Jacobshagen's journals. Keith is a fine landscape painter, and for more than thirty years he's been filling hardbound orange engineer's field books with drawings, watercolor sketches, and observations. I know from years of experience that keeping a journal is like taking good care of one's heart. Keith's journals are good medicine. They're beautiful, they're priceless, and I hope that some museum eventually has the good sense to acquire the entire collection. Young artists, young musicians, young writers, and museumgoers both young and old would find them inspirations, just as I have.

But instead of being jealous of the record that Keith's made of his life, I've put together my own little field book, in which I've included sketches and landscape studies made out of words, and thrown in a few observations about life. Keeping the original for myself, of course, I now offer a copy to you.

THE WHEELING YEAR

JANUARY

It's New Year's Day, and the future backs up, beeping with cheer, and closes its iron maw on the past. And then, with its massive hydraulics, it crushes the last year, mushing all the days together. Then it lumbers away, groaning and leaking, the scraps of the good times flapping farewell from the edges.

That flat snap of a stick match popping to flame on a cast iron stove lid, the first sound of the morning, and then the whoosh of the draft in the pipe, well, that's one of the most important noises of the past two hundred years, more so than the sweet peal of any victory bell, or the words of the greatest leader, and when you are lying in bed in the predawn darkness, fearing the future, that's the sound I recommend you listen for.

But why must I put on this old body day after day, sitting on the side of the bed, pulling on one leg and then the other, tucking the cuffs into my feet, pulling the top over my skull and then trying to smooth out the wrinkles? I'm an old fellow now, have paid off the mortgage and have a little money in the bank. I ought to be able to treat myself to a new body every few years, getting a tax receipt when I turn in the old one at the second-hand store.

Part of my morning ritual is to put on my shoes without sitting down, and by this demonstrating to myself that I am not so old as to topple over into a steaming heap when trying to balance on one leg. I even tie them that way, shoe in the air, wobbling on one leg and then the other, making a point of it.

Such pleasure there is in the simple, though, such as fitting the ball of my thumb into the bowl of a spoon, and the smooth bowl warming to my touch. Can it be that I have discovered that the first spoon was formed by a thumb? And to hold it like this, with the bowl between finger and thumb, its handle trembling just a little in my fingers, standing in my flannel nightshirt the first thing in the morning, how lovely it is.

If there's some one thing to live for, how can we choose just one among so many? Take, for example, this ordinary kitchen chair, nineteen pieces of wood, fifteen of them—the spindles and legs—turned on a lathe, the seat sawn from a plank and shaped with a scraper, some of the pieces drilled, all of them sanded, fitted together, adjusted, clamped, and glued, a good week's work for someone fifty years ago, the dust of that workshop long since settled onto the cobwebs, the cobwebs swept away, the broom worn down and gone. Five bucks at a yard sale. Any god would be happy to be given just one good chair like this, upon which the light of hundreds of mornings has rested like grace itself, but how long has it stood there next to the kitchen table, turning first one way and then another, waiting for someone to take a moment's notice?

One of my mother's Moser uncles had raised, from a seed, in a copper laundry boiler, a little lemon tree that as it had grown had twisted this way and that, trying to escape those bone-cold Iowa winters, though it stood in the warmest spot, a parlor window to the south, and was now and then turned so each little leaf got a taste of the sun.

Each summer it bore a handful of rock-hard, acorn-sized lemons, and her aunt would make one pie, lathered with sweet meringue to overpower that poor tree's sour reluctance, and all the relatives would be invited to their house to taste a little slice of miracle.

And, hey, now comes another day, towed by a pickup with yellow caution lights and a big WIDE LOAD banner on its bumper, a vague shape lumbering forward, wrapped in plastic. Perhaps it's only a morning on its way to where an afternoon can be rolled up by its side and bolted on. Who knows how many pieces of this life are up ahead crowding the road? Watch out. Pull over a little.

Everywhere at this moment women are cupping their hands the way this teenage girl at the bus stop cups hers, striking a match to light a cigarette as if dipping a portion of light from the wind, then swiftly lifting the glow to her lips though it leaks through her stubby fingers and wets her sharp chin. She tastes it, she swishes it around in her mouth, she rinses her teeth with the smoke. And she closes her eyes just as those other women are closing theirs and draws the red light into her breast and holds it there, burning with pleasure, while with one hand, which in her mind is now tapered, lovely and sophisticated, she shakes the last drop of fire from the end of the match.

How many moons have I been too busy to notice? Full moons, half moons, quarter moons facing those thousands of suns, watching them bringing the years up, one piece at a time. Even the dark phases of moon after moon, gray stoppers plugged into a starry sky, letting a little light leak out around the edges. By my reckoning, almost a thousand full moons have passed above me now, and I have been too busy and self-absorbed to be thankful for more than a few, though month after month they have patiently laid out my shadow, that velvety cloak that in the moonlit evenings waits for me.

As, in the dented spaceship of my seventies (shaking a little and leaking water), I travel the endless reaches of my ignorance, all of the books I haven't read, and never will, come rolling at me out of the dark like a hail of asteroids. And now and then an entire library, with a glowing trail of checkout slips, just misses hitting me by inches. On board I carry what I know, a few thin volumes, mostly how-to books, survival guides, and, for my ancient ship, a manual of parts with no address to use in ordering. Oh, yes, and a handful of things I wrote myself, stuffed into the cracks around my window, open onto time.

Thrust through the frozen mud, these mussel shells at the edge of the lake look like the shoulders of men on some workaday errand, wearing black overcoats with patches through which white lining shows.

Where were they going that day, hunched into the wind of water, when by mistake they turned a corner into the wrong street, not even given so much as a last look back?

Kick one loose and toe it over, and you'll see that the body is gone, having been lifted away, perhaps on snowy wings, leaving a shining, immaculate brightness.

The path through any night is narrow, like walking a shining rail, and the stars are a cold wind in your face. Stop anywhere and wait a moment, and you'll feel the universe slip past, a cloud of black leaves blown in the other direction.

A single starless winter night can seem to last a century or longer, and while we sleep, some great movement like Zoroastrianism—ponderous, foggy, but quick to catch on—may rise from conjecture, flourish, fall out of fashion, and pass. Wherever we look when we waken, we see the hoar frost, white, crystallized salts from the vast tide of its theses.

In awe and in utter ignorance we walk the cold, glittering path through the garden, finding a few leaves scattered before us, the curled shreds of mysterious scrolls. While we slept, each twig, each blade of grass was touched by an age we know nothing about. Stepping lightly, we pass beneath the ancient alabaster columns of trees that hold up nothing now but time.

Not every day of the new year's calendar is an empty box waiting for fortune to fill it. A few come seeded with promise, like "Partial Eclipse," but the rest of each month stands open, a sectioned paper carton like those for Christmas ornaments, now empty. In the old year's calendar, soon to be thrown away, a few splinters of glass lie in the carton's bottom (once bright ideas), and the rusting, bent hooks of old habits.

After many years, two old friends came visiting with gifts, small packages of stories wrapped in the crumpled tissue of age, purchased with tears in our distant past.

I wadded the wrapping and tossed it aside, then held each story to the light, a perfect miniature of something gone, and we laughed, and wept with laughter, the three of us together, as if no time had passed, no time at all.

And just when I remembered a wonderful story I wanted to tell, I looked around, and my friends were putting on the overcoats of age and stepping back into the past, and some of their stories were already misplaced amidst the busy clutter of the present.

And another of my friends has gone, a woman I loved, borne on a gurney into the past, trailing a comet's tail of tubes and instruments, all of us swept up in her orbit, then falling behind, tumbling through space, reaching for something to cling to, watching the past, a vast, glittering galaxy, drifting away.

In the long, low, ivory shafts of January light, a crow, alone on the melting ice of the river, follows its shadow, pecking at it, drinking it in.

FEBRUARY

Cold stove of 4:00 a.m., black iron, the lids in place on everyone but me, and down the chimney, through the damper's pinch, the distant hoo-hoo-hooing of an owl. And soon, among the sticks of kindling in the box of words, the mouselike scritching of my pen.

At times it seems I am in a slow revolving door, like those in airports, with spacious triangular chambers, and can turn and glance back through the heavy glass where the past is assembled, crowded with people, though I am alone in the present with almost too much air and all that's behind me sweeping me forward into the bright parking lot with its traffic and flags, my heart on its little black clattering rollers, one key in my pocket and thousands of vehicles all just alike, and I must find my own among them.

Maybe we carry too much through the door from the past, propped open with a broom that has swept up so much sentiment it has bent to the shape of its sweeping—like a stiff old floor-length skirt still waltzing—then across the wide porch where those we love, living and dead, sit rocking and talking, all drinking longnecks and laughing together, none of them offering help.

Then over the grass, box after box, to the rented U-Haul that is our life, already stuffed with all we haven't been able to part with, stale with dead dreams and packed so hastily we will never be able to get to the wisdom we lugged out early and loaded on first.

Twenty-nine dollars a day is the going rate, about what a person could live on if he had to, and the past is right there in the rearview mirror, following close, painted with slogans, its springs bent down from all we ever were.

A man pushes a hand through a coatsleeve, then squeezes the air and lets it go as if to assure himself the world feels no different out at the other end.

All winter, the trees have dipped sticky fingers into the wind, collecting particles of red and yellow floating there since last fall's leaf fall, then rolling these together into buds that blend these colors into orange, hard buds still slightly sticky from the making, and all this happens while we never notice.

Walking to work today, I came upon a maple leaf, or rather, a piece of red silk cleverly cut to resemble a maple leaf, something from an artificial bouquet, or perhaps from an artificial tree. It was skimming along on the ice in front of a barber shop, so light it scarcely touched the surface. Of course, I snatched it up and held its plastic stem to prevent it from flying on. Oh, it wanted to fly, all right, but its feeble struggles were no match for a man of a hundred and fifty pounds who has been finding things like this for many years. I've kept it here on my desk all day, sensing how far it has journeyed, this leaf like love itself, more light, more bright than it should ever be.

In the ditch by the road I found a crumpled letter almost as white as the snow that held it. It was the report of a paternity test, addressed to the father. The baby is a boy. This report had lain all winter in the hands of snow, slowly unfolding, opening to light and water, and the type had faded, but not quite enough.

The bed in the guest room of people I know is kept tightened and tucked, with bolstered pillows plumped and waiting, but this upstairs room gets little use, though this evening, for three or four hours, the winter coats of a dozen guests lay here as if on a raft borne up by waves of talk from below. Now the guests have gone into the glossy black fur of a starry night, the bedspread has been stroked and patted, and the room has returned to two dimensions as seen through the frame of the doorway, a photograph from *Architectural Digest* of the eternal and expectant present.

I drove my friend Stewart to the airport. He was going back to New York to die. He smiled and said, "Teddy, haven't we had a good time?" and I know he had. During his last half hour, I can imagine him hurrying in and out of a door, packing his battered Cadillac with what he wanted to keep from his sixty-one years, boxes with taped-up seams jammed full of those good times, a pillow case stuffed with successes, a jam jar of ideas for art, too good to let go, and a few Hawaiian shirts for sometime later. He left his big star paintings behind to light the empty room, then closed the door, turned up his collar, cranked the squealing v8 till it coughed and started, tuned in the radio to check on the weather for the rest of eternity, then snapped in his cassette of the last of the music.

At the end, though the soul may fly out, all of the shadows are drawn back into the body—shadows of young man and old, shadows that raced away over the grass. Even the casket handle leaves nothing behind but a cold white weight in the hand.

And six months later, into the void of that absence, like one of those metal containers they load on ships, we've packed the days that have survived you, friend, most of them ordinary as wadded up newspapers, or so it now seems, looking back. Yet you would have found much to amuse yourself among them, receiving each day with those old knotted hands and holding it before you like a gift.

The afterlife is probably what the geologists call a series of aftershocks—soft, fading tremors that follow months after a death, years after, making the hearts of those who survive swing just a little on the weakening ropes of their memories: the odd gait of a stranger that reminds us of someone we knew, a voice overheard in a crowd, the life left in an old coat at the back of a closet, and those who are gone who were good to us stay good, and are sweetly remembered, while those who were bad are punished and punished and punished as long as we live.

He presses his old face to the window and tries to find a friend's name among the shoals of others swimming by. Oh, he says, it'll come to me later, and it will, as the thousands of names that he knows bump up against the end of his life and flash and turn and bump against the beginning, back and forth, until the one he has been searching for finally passes close to his face, and catches the light, and he says the name aloud and smiles, as he stands with his bowl of oatmeal going cold, peering out through the kitchen window.

A drab brown duck turns upstream and effortlessly paddles against the chill current of time, the minutes smoothing her feathers and brightening them, her clear yellow eyes positioned to see to both sides, to forward and back. Just there she holds herself. Though I watch a long while, she never lets go.

This is an old woman's final illness, and the darkness that followed her seventy-nine years has slipped inside her now and has spread with cold fingers the blinds of her ribs.

It is not easy to see Death there waiting, sitting all day by the window, but at times a small shudder rattles the slats and shakes down the dust of a cough.

Don't talk to me about the stars, about how cold and indifferent they are, about the unimaginable distances. There are millions of stars within us that are just as far, and people like me sometimes burn up a whole life trying to reach them.

MARCH

Early in March, in the shadow of the abandoned Assembly of God, there's a melting snowdrift shaped like a hand whose five thin fingers reach to soothe the grass on the neighboring lawn. Each day this white hand shrinks back farther into the empty sleeve of the church.

After the kitchen had been cleaned, swept, mopped, and wiped with a rag and the rag draped over the tap, all that remained was the odor of the pilot light, a tiny blue crocus of flame that when called upon would light up all four of the burners under tomorrow. But now that too is gone, along with all of those tomorrows, its fluttery light replaced by the snap of a spark, though some of us may one day find its fragrance on a morning breeze and with a little whoosh of light the past will open like a flower.

This ant trap, this white steel pillbox with gun ports open in all four directions is not likely to draw in these tiny soldiers. They mill about the plaza of the countertop, stopping each other to ask directions. They want to take something sweet to the fat queen they love, who lies sweaty and pale in her curtained room.

In the crabapple tree by the side porch, four nestling robins, a tiny barbershop quartet, leans shoulder to shoulder, not quite ready for concert, but practicing hard, their heads thrown back, breasts puffed, beaks wide as they shape the one pitch they've been trying to get right all morning, squeezing their eyes shut over the effort. They want so much to be heard, but they have sustained that one note so long that it has lifted right out of them and vanished into the flowery crabapple shadows, leaving them gaping in silence.

Oh, my earnest birder friends, let me tell you that my grandmother's long Life List included an iron skillet, with its low scrape of a song; a stirring fork with worn tailfeathers; a heavy lid that nested on a pot and whistled, calling dozens of red potatoes up out of the garden; a gurgling, chirping percolator; as well as a number of other common local species, including the flying aroma of bacon. Her apron pockets were filled with the feathers of Kleenex, she kept a collection of big brown eggs in a wire mesh basket, and she wore a pair of powerful glasses that hung from her neck on a green and white plaid shoestring. Every day she was out in her kitchen watching and waiting, looking out from among the pots and pans, jotting her notes on hot dishwater, but in eighty years she was never to see the elusive, whirring Cuisinart, the Salad Shooter with its throaty cough, or the juicer with its sticky nest.

God knows what kind of stray it might be, some working breed, I'd guess, a hot black tangle of hair and twigs and leaves like a shadow still stinking of whatever cast it, a dark thing that someone scraped from the floor of the woods and left in a heap in our garage: damp throw rug, roll of mud. But whose brown eyes are these, peering so brightly out of the mystery, and whose pink tongue tip just touches the tips of my fingers? Oh, dog, oh, roaming thief of love, so joyfully I find you in your myriad disguises.

In the baby's fist is the first thing he owns, a little ball of air, but soon he tires of this and grabs another, then another after that.

So early in life we learn about more, and having more. In more it seems we have eternity, and for years we grasp and grasp, until one day we find that we have less. And then life goes and goes, it floats away, and at the end we find our hand is empty, but for one small ball of air.

Driving at night, sometimes a star comes right up out of nowhere and, for a minute or two, leaves itself there at the end of the road, twinkling and flashing, and then the star slides sidewise, slowly, becoming a plane, a big plane with its headlights on, full of hundreds of people talking together. We drive along in silence, you and I, not speaking of so small a thing. It happens all the time.

There are millions of pieces of the cross, all over the world. This one looks like a piece of plaster lath and is holding a window open, airing a room that has been closed too long.

We come prepared to lose, and at the end Death takes the pot, all of the chips—red, white, and blue—his soft white hands, with rings on every finger, raking his winnings from the bright green field. His big black Caddy is parked out front, and in it is someone else's wife.

The lost billfold was there all along, of course, lying in under the car, its breathing shallow, a clam with its brown hinge polished by wear, its halves closed tightly over the pearly credit cards. Under a streetlamp starry with moths, you stand in the steady boat of your shadow at two in the morning, cheerlessly thumbing its crumpled green gills.

My wife, the newspaper editor, starts while still standing in bathrobe, socks, and glasses, sweeping the newspaper up and snapping it flat the way the wind snaps a bedsheet hung on a line, and her gaze is a steady wind as she settles into her chair, the sharp and earnest wind of March, getting in under the leaves of the words and turning them over and over, then letting them tumble and skip into drifts in her wake, fresh arrangements of news for the day's attention.

Dust has been scuffed or rubbed or scratched from the flesh of the globe and carried on winds that blew through every history. In our time it is drawn to computers. It beats its wings against their snowy screens as if the internet, which promises so much, might let it in.

That wristwatch, that little gauge you wear, the one you worry over, the one that shows the pressure rising in the boiler of your life? Why not quit reading it? Just open a valve and whistle.

Howard, my yellow lab, has lugged a heavy cow bone up from some cleft in the pasture and left it on the lawn like a rolled up Sunday paper, its news almost completely gnawed away by weather, though one can read a little of it: how the hoofprints of her sisters brimmed and stank with muddy water and the flies were like sparks in her eyes. And in almost every paragraph it seems that grass is mentioned, like a prayer. But Howard has tired of the lowing woes of a cow's last report, dried out and hollow now, and has fallen asleep. He dreams of a bone cracked open before him, the violent language of marrow, like licking the red from a sunset.

On the shoulder, an orange caution sign flaps on a flimsy tripod. We come upon bag after plastic bag, dropped by the road by litter pickup volunteers and soon we fly swiftly upon them, young people and old, bent over their work and shouting back and forth, ears cupped against the shuddering rush and chill and whistle of passing trucks, the thousand quick hands of the wind feeling about in their jackets. Some of them are conversing; others are walking alone, heads down, lost in their thoughts. Everybody is there. Everybody but us. We pass without slowing and drop them behind like empty bags to blow up into their own tight fences, then to break free and fly on.

Here, in the rag bag, is a poppy from somebody's sundress, but now it smells like all the other rags.

Imagine this bluestem as salt grass, and these crows as a species of gull, and you will know what it's like to live on the coast of the sky, waves of light slapping the barns, splashing the windows with a blue that has come all the way from the other side.

You've seen the way in which a woman chooses a dress from her closet, then stands before a mirror, holding it at arm's length, clutching its shoulders as if it were a son she is sending to war, looking him up and down and then drawing him close and pressing him against her breast. And then she sees herself embracing him, and smiles, the two of them looking so perfect together, full of such hope, facing the future.

APRIL

All this talking, all these raindrops interrupting each other. *But but but,* they say, so earnest, so eager to please. But not one offers a good explanation, not one can answer the one big question, though I patiently listen, sitting in thin gray morning light, another day before me.

Month of my birth. What record do we poets leave? Not on stone tablets, but in books like leaves that have matted together under the snows of indifference. That we were fretful, mostly, but that now and then we looked up and glimpsed something wonderful passing away.

Early in April I sometimes hear from deep in the woods the watery burble of a wild tom turkey as he beckons his harem, and I have seen them stepping so carefully across the colorful tiles of the leaves, brown shawls over their shoulders, bobbing their heads as if obedient, submissive, but catching each other's bright willful eyes.

The passing years have broken this old sidewalk over the knees of tree roots, those of great maples raining shade, and of crippled elms whose leaves in August turn to a lace that sifts the heat. And the breaks have filled with mold from which frail seedlings, already with bark like their parents, hold up green banners of hope.

For sixty or maybe seventy years this sidewalk has been lying here, literally under foot, and suddenly, one morning when you look, it's there, supporting you, its every pebble like a jewel—yellow or brown or red or black—set in the sandy concrete, ants patching their old gray tent.

Such happiness there is in being a part of all this, of dismissing the woman watching from her window while I bend to one knee to press my hand against this broken sidewalk, feeling the light of that same sun that the sparrow hops over, and that warms the cricket as it carries its song across town in its purse.

After a long illness, rain idly brushes the roof with the back of its hand. Only the fingernails touch, and they touch ever so lightly. I remember a woman who late one evening talked to me about dying, about how easy it might be, and as she talked she very slowly turned her hand palm up and let it relax as if to catch something falling out of the darkness.

Her hair was white, a cloud, and her eyes were the transparent green of leaves with sunlight showing through. It seemed that I was peering into her to find whatever might be hidden, singing there. And as she cut my hair, for that is how she made her living, she told me that in a cardboard box in the back room she had two orphaned birds, a tiny Steller's jay and another still too small to properly identify. She planned to feed and care for them until they were ready to fly, for that is what, she said, she did for love. We talked through the mirror, where I sat in her nest, under the folded wings of a barber's cloth, eyes wide and bright, my shiny old man's beak between them, a woman feeding me with words.

The twenty-five-cent photo booth has disappeared, poof, along with the five-and-dimes they'd found a corner in, as with the boys and girls who stepped inside and drew the curtain, light as time, across their grins and mischief. Such fun it was to step out into the glaring light of the rest of your life, carrying your face as it had been framed for just that instant, your smile like a joke, the really good joke of a kisser as young as it would ever be again, frozen in black and white and damp with chemicals, fixed in a cold tin frame.

For a girl pouring water into the cappuccino machine from a spotted carafe at the Quik Stop at eight in the evening, an old man is as difficult to look at as a page of homework. On the counter next to the register, her geometry book lies heavy, brown, and unopened. Her notebook has phone numbers scribbled all over the cover. What's the point in learning to be old, she is thinking, when that is something she will never have to use?

At the automated checkout machine at the public library, the book gets a very hard kiss as it leaves, the machine's big teeth fiercely pressed to the book's tight lips as if she might never return, and with this embrace comes the thunk of a slap on the back, enough to knock the words right out. Then the machine steps back in his steel-gray suit and holds his hands open as if to say "You will always be welcome," while the book, feeling hot and sticky in her clear plastic raincoat, turns and rushes away, desperate to wipe off her mouth.

This weathered stile stands alone in the field, its worn boards stepping up and over a fence that has long since fallen away—a good fence once, that grass is getting the better of now. But the stile is still responsible for bridging its part of the world, and the will of its wood gets harder and harder, here in the sun, in its drab gray uniform, one leg on each side of the border.

Writer and reader, we share so much. When I write *trellis*, I count on you seeing the flimsy slats tacked into squares and painted white, like a French door propped in a garden with a blue condensed from many skies pressed up against the panes. I count on you knowing that remarkable blue of the morning glory shaped into the fluted amplifying horns of Edison cylinder record players. What? Come on, you know exactly what I'm talking about. I didn't need to describe them like that, but I like to hover a little over my words, dabbling the end of my finger in the white throats of those _____. You fill it in. I could go on, but all I really needed to do was to give you the name of the flower. I knew you'd put in the rest, maybe the smell of a straw hat hot from the sun; that's just a suggestion. You know exactly what else goes into a picture like this to make it seem as if you saw it first, how a person can lean on the warm hoe handle of a poem, dreaming, making a little more out of the world than was there just a moment before. I'm just the guy who gets it started.

At first light we find the fog in faded denim overalls lying on its side a few yards from the house. How big it is! Has it lain there all night like some old drunk, come home to find the cold door bolted and all of us asleep inside? And on one knee a patch, all right, a red one, big as the barn.

This patch of phlox is a bright, delighted blue this April morning, as one by one they open their petals to find to their great surprise that the three old Norway pines that each spring shaded them have disappeared over the winter, having succumbed to the tiny pine blight beetle, leaving only their weeping stumps, some oily sawdust and chips, and a scatter of needles and cones.

If a flower can pray, and if a patch that stands together prays together, spring after spring, then this is their miracle answer, a field of dazzling light, where trees have been replaced by flowers.

An old bachelor settled a row of stones the size of laying hens along the driveway, digging a shallow nest for each, then dabbled them chalky white with leftover housepaint, and every April, after he'd gotten his garden in, he'd touch them up, down on his swollen knees with a paintbrush stiff as a paddle that dripped a trail of sticky white from stone to stone, all the way out to the road, as he got the grand entrance ready for someone who might one day just stop to say hello.

In a paper carton sealed with tape, his ashes wait in darkness just behind his name and dates on a marble door. Surely this can't be the special package the future's been waiting for.

At day's end one page from the ancient book of sunsets blazes and smokes on a fire that has burned forever, yet is not warm enough to keep us young.

This night is a cold, deep lake, and I am lying on its bottom, surprised to be able to breathe. The bellied sail of the moon has been wafted out of sight, but thousands of starlights sparkle up there on the surface, just bright enough that I can hold up the fish of my fingers and watch them dart this way and that, hungrily feeding on the darkness. Who could be happier to be alive than I?

MAY

When at last the light from the next galaxy arrives, or what is left of it arrives, it is only a speck, the pinpoint center of what was once an enormous snowball of light, come rolling down the black tarpaper roof of the universe, losing itself all the way, nine hundred thousand years of loss, only enough left of it to light one facet of a grain of sand, here at the edge of a Quik Stop parking lot in Omaha.

I found it once, a marble marker yellowed by sequins of lichen, no bigger than a family Bible lying face up in deep grass near a country road, the inscription so softened by rain I had to read it with my fingers, the only headstone in a weedy square so small that a dozen fence posts had been enough to parcel it off from fields stretching into forever.

The grave is still there, of course, now hidden in what in the intervening thirty years has grown up in trees and briars. Today I'd have to crawl to find it, pulling myself through the leaf mold under the juniper boughs, through the thorny plums, and even then I probably couldn't find it, sunken under a matting of grass. Even the last of that lost name is surely gone.

Asleep on her side, with tangled hair stuck to her face, this girl on a bench is like the lost sailor alone in a boat, tossed on the waves in that painting by Winslow Homer, while the shark of the afternoon sun shows his great yellow eye.

Freshly clipped grass from the mown shoulder blows over the highway, swirling under the passing traffic, a rippled, meandering river of green, too shallow to carry anything but light, the pebbles of the speckled bottom shining through. It is this easy stream, this afternoon, these greens upon greens the meadowlark has captured in a few clear notes, one flute against an orchestra of wind, and through it all, a yellow center line.

Gathering wild mushrooms with friends, the sun's hands helping us up and down the banks of a creek, I stumbled upon a tiny green pennant fluttering over the dead black leaves, a clue, it seemed, purposefully placed there for me, and by which, for an instant, I was able to make my way into the past, and to hear my young mother saying its name—no, *giving* me its name—jack-in-the-pulpit—that I might say it all my life: first, silently to myself with a kind of elation, then calling it out to my friends.

On its edges, the part called the selvage, the fabric is more tightly woven to prevent it from fraying, and for us, it's the fingers, a fringe at the edge, that get the most wear, touching then drawing away.

I have seen the vendors of cotton candy walk like bouquets of pink light to the end of the midway and back selling blossoms like those of these May peonies, which are so quickly consumed, snatched by the sun's hot fingers, leaving a clutter of petals like empty paper cones.

A storm swept through in the night with lightning crashing at its leading edge and a soft rain trailing behind, and it came to me as

I lay awake that somebody's life was passing by, the fireworks of youth out in front and, in the middle years, a sweet rain, steady, brimming the rusting buckets. After it passed, there came a chill that shook the brittle, spotted leaves. By morning, the sky was cloudless and the grass in the yard had sprung back. The lane was untracked, as far as I could see.

Oh, melancholy, how poor I would be without you drawing my attention to this or that. Yesterday it was the wild plum blossoms along the brief road to today, and today it's this rain that will rain only once. Each grain of sand on each shingle lights for an instant, like a window across a black lake, and then the tiny shade is drawn, as time strikes the wet panes and glances away. Tomorrow, too, you will be waiting with something to show me. That time, for example, when you dipped a spoon into the plain water of an ordinary day, then lifted it, salty with tears, to my lips.

With a few raps of his hammer the plumber loosened the joint and the long, sour life of the rust gave way with a feeble cry. Then setting his boots just so, he gripped the pipe in the wrench of his fist, pulled it away, and held it at arm's length as if it were a banister he'd just torn from a wall, then dropped it with a clang, defying the silence.

And maybe half of the climb up the steep steps of his life, he rested, took off his cap, found his face, and rubbed it, feeling his bones with his hand, the bones feeling his fingers, then set his face forward into the light from the top of the stairs.

Beside a highway, a man in a straw hat sits in a canvas chair with a clipboard, and on it a counter with which he is counting the cars, tapping again and again, like the bell on a hotel desk, but no clerk arrives with a key, for the rooms in the clouds have all been taken.

The motors of the two tall locusts next to the house have been running all day with the steady, unfaltering hum of an attic fan, stirring the soft May air, powered by a current of bees, thousands of them that have been beckoned into the almost invisible lacy brown flowers by a nectar far too high in the branches for those of us below to taste, at least in this world.

Female cottonwoods, no longer welcome in the cities because of their wispy, drifting seed, live on in the small prairie towns, old giants with drab gray overcoats thrown open to show off their lightning scars, limbs broken and hanging, creaking as they swing. Tarry spit of tobacco-yellow buds, raspy chuckle of leaves. And in early June, the seeds ride a whisper of breeze, gathering among the oily engine parts and wrenches in the open-doored repair shops, or resting in front of the barber shop, or pressing up against a widow's window screens.

Four in the morning, and the bullfrogs are rearranging furniture, shoving it over the floor of the darkness, the planks groaning and groaning under the weight. A lot of hard work, but worth it when at dawn they lift their eyes just above the cool shine of the water and see children appearing at windows, enchanted by everything new.

Over the centuries we've weighed the roses down with so much sentiment and lore that some have simply given up and disappeared, taking their hues and fragrances, and leaving behind, engraved in copperplate in books with flaking leather bindings, their fading images and those Latin names they never asked for anyway. Only those dowdy old aunts, the floribundas, come back spring after spring to stand nodding beside the gravestones, clutching damp wads of pink Kleenex, and sighing in puffs of perfume.

At the cemetery on the edge of town, a big bald nephew, restrained from dashing back to his farm by the leash of a necktie, opens the trunk of his Dodge, takes out a wheelchair, and snaps it open like a carton.

From the back seat he lifts an old woman, dressed in navy, with hair that flares like a dandelion going to seed. He tucks her in and sets her shoes on the metal flippers.

This is a man used to dragging heavy things with wheels over bumpy ground—dollies of seed bags, welding carts—and instead of pushing her over the grass, he pulls her backward, head tipped and bobbing, her eyes looking back at the path she's been on eighty years, leading straight to this grassy hill with its twisted cedars, overlooking the fields.

They have covered the pile of dirt beside the grave with plastic turf, a green like that of moss at the foot of a rotting tree trunk, and beside it there he lies, her husband of sixty years, sealed in a gleaming walnut casket, afloat on the black canvas straps of the lowering machine, his eyes closed over his half of the memories.

Something like the Great Depression goes on and on, year after year, and many of us who weren't even born in the thirties have seen clouds of grasshoppers darken the sun and rain down over our lives, eating the handles off our marriages. We've seen the wells of hope dry up and have choked on the drifting dust of advice. We've loaded what was left of us—sad-sack, failed, and foreclosed—on the roof and running boards and lumbered away on patched tires, swallowing pride, waving good-bye to the neighbors. Red-eyed and weepy, we've peered through dirty windshields into the miles to the end of our lives, trying to believe, along with Ma Joad toward the end of *The Grapes of Wrath*, we'll be all right 'cause we're the people.

There were parts of herself that were not in the mirror and those were pretty: a kindly touch inside the gloves of her big red hands, a well of patience behind her ropy eyebrows, and a love of children under the knocking bones of her breast. It was these he admired, while she could see him needing her behind that freshly shaven face with a cleft in its chin in which black whiskers grew beyond a razor's reach.

Rather than drink from the stream, my dog prefers her water from my hands, and so I set aside my pretensions, and become a leaky bowl.

Some of our houses have pink fiberglass insulation, like soft sunrises floating up under their roofs, while others have thunderheads sodden with news: the daily papers chewed into a gray confetti as if by time itself—a thick storm of ill fortune through which the attic wiring runs crackling with lightning.

Old horseshoe pits. Step gently over these sunken graves marked only by stakes pounded deep in the prairie. Generations of iron clanging on iron lie buried in their sandy silences.

We see only the moon's fixed face, as you know. It never turns aside in pain, in anger or disgust. It is thus the good parent, holding the earth at arm's length, gripping its shoulders with cool white hands, turning and turning around it as if it were saying good-bye, as if it were taking one last long look. But the moon with its homely, familiar face, has been wishing that we fare well every evening for millions of years, fully knowing that we would be there in the morning, ready to try.

Many of those communities were never towns, just names that little groups of immigrants gave to the empty land they settled, dreaming that hard work, faith, and fortune might one day bring them at least a crossroads store, a place to pick up the mail and talk with neighbors about their children, the crops, and weather.

Paplin was like that, set in a valley in Howard County, Nebraska, with a clapboard church, a parochial school, and dreams and wishes. And up a grassy hill was a plain farm gate that, summer and winter, swept the nodding grass to let the bereaved, with wagons and teams, enter the hilltop graveyard to bury their dead, for the most part Polish Catholics whose graves are marked by crosses lifted to the blue eternity of prairie skies.

If you stand there under the creaking cedars you can see for more than a hundred years.

During the weeks, because it was too far to walk each day, or to drive a wagon and team, the children stayed at the parish schoolhouse, sleeping on mats on the floor, attended by nuns.

In the winter of 1892, as the story goes, one little boy came down with diphtheria and brought it to school, and by that spring, nearly a hundred children had died, the better part of a generation. There are three long rows of gently rolling sod along the fence line, overlooking the church, marked only by a cross with no inscription as if all words had failed, a plain stone cross the size of a six-year-old with arms outstretched to embrace the future. Someone who still remembers their story has fastened a few blue plastic flowers into the fence.

JUNE

Bumper to bumper, the days stream past the day-old baked goods store though sometimes a Sunday morning pulls in, driven by some old man who stops in the present for a moment to buy a little bag of yesterdays. But mostly the days, by the dozen, dry out and get thrown to the birds, sparrows and starlings to whom each hour is every bit as tasty as the last.

Time and again, our parents cautioned us that quicksand was waiting just under the water to suck us right out of the world, and, though we fooled with finding it, not one of us did. It was all imagination, for the bottom was always solid under us as, barefoot and lucky, we waded the summers. But more than the bottom, it was time that firmly held us up, all of us young and calling back and forth above the surface.

The heron I have disturbed on my walk awkwardly lifts from her place at the edge of the pond, slapping the water, and flaps into the woods without a single word though I have driven her away from a soup of minnows floating in a silver bowl.

And from their chosen spots along the bank, where all morning they have been angling for dragonflies, relishing those tangy blues, one after another the great bullfrogs dive under their tattered tablecloth of duckweed with no more than a squeak of frustration.

The little garter snake that wriggles away writes not one angry word in her peculiar cursive, nor does the black wasp curse though she must drop her pellet of mud and fly, and the cabbage moth, disturbed at her meal of broccoli leaves, flutters away but is able to hold her long tongue. Each of them wordless, waiting for me to be gone.

This dumpster can't go far on those sore little wheels that have such a hard time making it over the broken cement. It is like a fat old man (or fat old woman), who has to be helped both into and out of a chair, by a lumbering son or daughter heaving with effort. And for clothes the standard coverall brown or blue with bleached-out spots. And a voice like a clank, mouthing the same complaint over and over, with very bad breath, down there in the flies at the end of the alley.

During the night, the cleaning staff has come and gone, moving invisibly in and out of the empty offices, leaving new phone books, gleaming in shrink-wrap, and taking the old ones down the hall to the coffee room to stack them soft and exhausted beside the water cooler. For an hour, alone at my desk, I thumb through the new book, turning leaves to find you gone—and you, and you, and you—no longer listed, missing, swept away. All day, the old books, ruffled by wear, lean in their sorry pile, until at closing time, a man with a squealing handcart arrives to wheel them away. He passes my door with his load of old names, rolling away.

Many have never noticed the Unknown Soldier there on the courthouse lawn, squinting from under the bill of his cap into time, which is nothing but light.

Carrying briefcases, hoping for justice, the living walk past, heads bowed. This young attorney in her dark suit with a silk scarf white as a document knotted about her long neck? Let's wish her well, whatever her brief, that word so right in the sight of a mildewed monument like him. She hasn't looked up, nor reached out to brush with her bright red fingertips the soldiers' names on his pedestal. He stands with his stone knees locked, one hand on his rifle, the other saluting the distance, and she is the distance.

What am I offered for this shoebox of tools? Do I hear a half dollar?

This was her hammer. On its handle, these spatters of cream and yellow paint are all that is left of her kitchen walls and the trim for the two small windows, one that opened south to her vegetable garden, one that looked east to a neighbor's yard. Cream enamel for the sunny sill upon which her pill bottles stood, expired prescriptions to the left and the most recent ones to the right. And these yellow spots are for the wall upon which, in sequence, hung sixty years of glossy travel calendars, free from the funeral home.

And this was her only screwdriver, the wooden handle taped together and part of the tip snapped off, perhaps from prying open a can of paint.

This roll of electrical tape is worth a quarter all by itself, and here's an assortment of faucet washers you'd have to pay a dollar for at Coast to Coast, and look what else:

These were her pliers, the rivet gone, fixed with a bolt she had to tighten in order to cut up a coat hanger for wire to replace the wire that rusted through and dropped her wren house out of the birch, a tree that later died, as birches are known to, of rot from too much rain, and which for a week, in coat and scarf, she tried to cut up with this worthless keyhole saw, bought at a yard sale for a dime and not worth even that, with its untempered, cheap little blade that bent and then had to be bent back and then just bent and bent again until it was too soft to saw. And then she had to pay the neighbor five dollars to chainsaw up the tree and do it not even half as well as she said she could have done it herself, had she been willing to pay fifteen dollars and ninety-five cents to buy a fancy saw she might not need again, and didn't, as it happened.

The hammer, the electrical tape, the assortment of faucet washers, a pair of still useable pliers, and let's throw in the little keyhole saw. The handle's good. You can buy a blade at your Coast to Coast. Just look at all of this you're getting.

Who'll give a nickel for the works?

One day a woman picked a small thing from the world she knew, a bunch of blue forget-me-nots, and carefully embroidered them onto the edge of a part of a world that would go right on without her, this pillowcase that once, rinsed fresh with blueing and pinned on her clothesline, must have been bright as a window thrown open on the moon, and felt like pressing her cheek to a garden of stars. This morning, priced for a quarter on a table of linens that stands in her yard, it has been folded flat, like the flag of the country of flowers.

I like the word *locket*, its sure finality, its hollow snap like heart-shaped hands clapping shut on a photograph, a piece of confetti, one little round face that came floating down out of a sky full of faces above the parade of a life. And sometimes, clipped into that past, you discover—faint, as from a great distance—a tinny brass band of perfume.

I give you this ingot of sunbeams, this bale of straw, dusty with earth, that rode all day on the back of a wagon, scattering chaff. Drunk on the late afternoon light, it sleeps like a horse while the moon creeps into the legs of its trousers.

One can never relax in the presence of gold, so self-absorbed it is, but one can lie down next to a straw bale any old time, as if it were a brother.

Still alive, on the shore of everything he's ever known, an old man stands at a window overlooking a sea of grass. He is wearing the faded pajamas of dreams, in one of which a dear uncle, forty years dead, lay dying all over again, his ivory fingers pinching feathers of light from his bedsheet. But here there is more light than anyone could hope to gather, a wrinkled sheet of dazzle, and thousands and thousands of minutes washing to shore.

In a stack by the back door of the locked-up Goodwill store, a dozen jigsaw puzzles wait to be carried in, each box with a landscape on its lid, the top one with a snowy peak reflected in a lake, each one assembled once and then left among the bags of shoes and shirts, the heavy chair with coffee-stained upholstery where someone sat to piece something together, starting in from the corners, one piece at a time.

Under orders, the junebugs throw themselves at the lighted window again and again, the privates, the corporals, the sergeants, even the second lieutenants. What must it be like to have light as your enemy, light with its numberless armies, bivouacked for the night in defensible houses, a camouflaged sniper lying on every leaf of every houseplant, watching you fail and fall back? Whose stupid idea was it to do it this way? Why not attack in the morning, when light is out in the streets, lusty and swaggering, and you can sometimes catch it boxed in at the end of an alley?

In your soft black sleep mask you enter the trust and savings of sleep. You force the guard to open the vault where dreams are kept and to give you the keys to the boxes. In one you find a silver charm bracelet of clocks and skulls and tiny shoes. You put on the shoes and start to run on dead legs back into wakefulness, where you find yourself sitting exhausted, carrying nothing but light on your hands.

In my Service and Maintenance Department, I keep my old mistakes, wiped clean with WD-40 and wrapped in rags. Every few days, I take down a few and check for rust or other signs of deterioration. The biggest are too heavy to lift, so I keep them on pallets, covered with tarps. The embarrassments are a little more fragile, so I keep them packed in bubble wrap in cartons in the vault. I have so many regrets that I have recently ordered new shelving.

Dead for a dozen years, Mr. Bob Ross, you live on in the TV reruns, permed hair like a bee swarm, big hands, big smile, a kindergarten-teacher voice. Show us again that little tree you say likes it right there by the moonlit path and the moon you tell us is just real happy right next to the mountain. Hundreds of thousands of us have waited to watch you at your easel, holding your magic brushes—the fan brush for clouds, the fitch for rocky peaks. Come back, keep coming back, Bob Ross. We need to know that everything is happy where it is, and that we too might put it there.

It takes only a little overnight rain to start the bullfrogs' foghorns droning out in the mist, in the bent wet grass banking the pond. It is almost the sound of a bass key struck again and again by the blind piano tuner, Fred Cushing, as he sat at the buzzy old upright in the stale-beer back of the Silver Spur Lounge in Ames, smoking a Pall Mall, fifty years ago. Even that name, Pall Mall, sounds like his stubby, nicotine-yellow finger, tapping again and again on that one flat note, tuning the yellow keys of the years.

If these great plains were a dance floor, these clouds strung above would be the paper lanterns, with pale flutters of lightning inside.

Moonglow, the soft sax of an evening breeze, and in the distance (fifty years back in the distance) Kim Novak and William Holden, holding each other in *Picnic* and turning and turning under the stars.

Or maybe these clouds are only a handful of dance wax lifting like dust from the road.

JULY

Last night, in the distance, the pops and toothy whistles of rockets, booms of bombs, and strings of firecrackers rattling like rocks in a can. This morning, taking a walk at the lake, the revelers gone, the parking lot littered with flattened, dewy silence, red and gray, the hollow tubes, the burned-out cones, and all the duds, their fuses hissing right up to the edge of a bang that never arrived. All gone silent now, the sighs, the expectations, irritations and regrets, only the chirr of hundreds of swallows darting and diving, picking the last bits of smoke from the air.

After the fireworks, tall palm trees of smoke drifted north on the wind, a floating island, ghostly, disappearing. But this was an illusion; it was we who were passing, standing together on the lawn, leaving an evening behind.

The fisherman's shadow falls headlong into the stream, but the water pays no attention, makes no attempt to carry it off though it weighs less than a bobber, less than that soaked black leaf somersaulting along on the bottom, or that grain of sand stumbling behind. All afternoon his shadow swims against the current, growing so weak that by nightfall the least ripple can sweep it away.

There are few perfect things in this world, and one of them is your common, everyday pound of butter, cool in its box, printed in blues and greens with pleasant images—a farm, a farmer, a cow at a fence—and divided into quarters wrapped in immaculate paper as neatly tucked and folded as a soldier's bunk, each section as easy to slide in and out as if riding on soundless rollers, like drawers in filing cabinets, two two-drawer cabinets placed side by side, the files packed in, manila, clean and fresh,with evenly spaced dividers arranged by the tablespoon. To press it to your cheek and then, with a fingernail, to carefully lift the triangular folds at each end, one end at a time, and then, without tearing the paper, to open the final flap and find there butter, yellow, pure, and flawless, too good to be true.

There's the ghost of a man still standing in these golf shoes here on a waist-high, thrift store shelf that bends just a little under his weight and opinions. His head's in the shadowy, dusty upper shelves, in a country club of nail-hung tennis and handball rackets and under a Panama hat, disapproving of me. Big man, big leathery-smelling feet in their dried-out white buck golf shoes, fancy brown fringed tongues like the leaves of neglected plants. All variegated, too, with burn-like grooves from the suffering laces.

I sit on the floor, leaned up against a stack of books, and slip them on. How smooth their insides are, shiny from years of loose wear. It's like slipping right into his feet, into his life, and now I can I hear him above me, bellowing with outrage that someone like me, so not so country club, would presume to put them on.

In this jar, just the weight of a heart, we have dark sorghum molasses, from an old woman's hot sorghum patch next to a slough. Delicious in cookies, on pancakes, or cornbread. All natural ingredients: the waxy light that slides from willow leaves, the clatter of frogs, the invisible territory carved out of the summer and claimed by a red-winged blackbird, yellow clay from the sole of a comfortable shoe, itch of a chigger bite, light footfall of woodtick, a little flour from a cotton apron, the grassy fragrance of an old straw hat, arthritis, diabetes, high blood pressure, a few muttered judgments on neighbors, and the hard rubber tip from a cane.

We are enjoying a light rain this morning, very rare these days, and people around here will be saying that, well, it didn't amount to much but was enough to settle the dust. Settling the dust with a soft rain like this can be a whole day's work for the weather, who gets paid by the job.

Here in the farm store's parking lot, between two pickups, is a tiny teeter-totter painted green, but no, it's a praying mantis, with the bulk of its weight parked round and fat on the low end of the balance. It's the only insect that can turn its head, but this head is not turning. In fact nothing about it is moving; it might be dead for all we know, we three who stand above it, strangers with shopping bags. It might have fallen off somebody's radiator and landed like this, on all six feet, as dead as a derrick. I think we'd wait forever, if we had the time, to see if it would move just a little, would turn its head with an eye like a dolphin to acknowledge us, we three who are all just a little afraid of any strangeness, even one so small.

Heat lightning: at the horizon, July in heavy boots paces the hot floor of the darkness. A bulb in a wobbly lamp jiggles. Or is that you, my friend, approaching across the firefly hills, swinging a sloshing pail of moonlight?

In the pasture, each grass blade is bent into or over the next, a complex system of triangles like the girders of old iron bridges riveted in place by frost, through which a mouse can cross, in relative safety, from one little island of life to the next.

Foolish, I stood in the bow of my shadow, my long black canoe, trying to see all the way to the mouth of the river where time runs out, and gulls skim over the surface, filling their bellies with the silvery breaths of the dying. Sit down, I told myself; your shadow can suddenly turn over, pitching you into the undertow. Sit down, I said again, you'll be there soon enough. Trust in your shadow to carry you there.

In front of a store I saw a man in slacks, white shirt, and necktie, cranking a canvas awning down, using one hand, twirling the crank in an expert way as down and down the awning creaked until it took him into its shadow, and at that moment, his free hand reached into the light as if to waggle his fingers in it before it was gone, but then I saw that he was only waving at a passing driver who waved back, pulled down his visor, and drove on.

The train of progress no longer stops at my station, but I watch it rush past, whistling. Nearly always, in one of the windows, I glimpse someone I know, in profile, lifting a styrofoam cup, reading the morning paper. But it is not to see my old friends passing that I get up early and sit here with paper and pen. I wait to see what progress will disturb. For example, this morning a damp newspaper from more than fifty years ago blew up into my face, fragrant with soil and geraniums from Decoration Day, and also the strong dark urine of my grandmother's bull terrier, Fiji.

After a 150-year journey in a sloshing hold, then jounced by wagon over cobbled and crowded portside streets, then rocked in a windy, rackety train through days of smoke and nights of sparks, this camel-backed trunk has come to rest in the dusty depot of an attic in Iowa, where little moves, where each morning the sun, its windows flashing, steams slowly out and away, taking new generations to the frontier.

Take any old pebble, dull and dusty, just part of a road, and moisten it with spit, and all of its colors will awaken, as if you'd kissed the life back into it, as if it had been waiting for someone like you.

It's only a weathered wood-duck house crudely hammered together from planks and nailed on a tree, and after more than twenty years of waiting it has never attracted a duck. But out of this minor embarrassment—a tale that will never be sung by the fire on winter nights, much less live on for centuries—it has warped and cracked and gained something in character, so that, like any old man or old woman, it appears to have something to say.

The most beautiful flowers of courage are not seen in the showy, loose petalled bouquets of our leaders, enormous gardenias perfuming whole banquet rooms. No, they are blossoms like this: a child-sized young woman with a homely face, alone on a seat on the city bus, eyelashes thick with mascara, lipstick smudged onto her small, determined mouth.

At the clothesline sale, a strapless bridesmaid's dress—tight folds of peach organdy gravelled with pearls—hangs like a teacup, dark stains where its lip fit under the arms of the owner. It's for sale for just fifteen dollars, but who could fill it again with that brew of excitement? And, for that matter, who could now timidly reach, on harshly whispered cue, all the way from the sleeve of this peach tuxedo into the bridesmaid's damp hand?

Five hundred feet up, in the cool, clear Saturday afternoon air above the lake there's a tiny cocklebur of noise towing a parachute, red, yellow, and blue, and it's Dennis Bowers, whom I know best with our weight side by side on the ground at St. Andrew's Episcopal Church, all four of our sore knees heavy as stones on the kneelers. But just now he's up there wrapped in a robe of pure delight as he slowly turns his silken prayer to avoid a dozen pelicans, angel-white, who will not change their course for him.

A gusty early summer wind reaches in and out of the maple, taking up armloads of leaves and feeling through them, then putting them back, like a woman with clothes in a dryer, a big woman in shoes with thin soles stepping as lightly as a dancer.

Pushed back from the table and left at odd angles, these six chrome chairs with red vinyl seats look like parts from a carnival ride. They're part of what's left of the morning coffee hour.

The street door stands open, and through the screen the laughter and *have-a-good-days* of businessmen blow in across the floor like crumpled napkins. They are going back to work, while behind them a few grains of sugar tumble past cups and spoons, then drop off the edge and into the rest of the day.

For three or four years, the cow skull lay by the gate where I left it one day, bringing it up from the field just to have carried home something out of the dust and the heat.

By autumn, the grass had accepted it. In one of its eyes was a soft, white cocoon.

Then it was spring, and the skull lay like the last of a snowdrift, dirty and gray.

Summers and winters, I counted on it being there. But today, walking in from the field, I bent there and pushed back the grass and found it gone. Some stranger, I'd guess, who, finding it, took it away, wanting a piece of the country. A skull doesn't care where it goes.

Run over and flattened on a country road, this dead frog looks like a fancy ornamental hinge, perhaps to a trapdoor hidden under the gravel. We wouldn't want to open it on all that blackness. And now a small brown moth alights on the pin of the dead frog's spine and with a tiny creaking, opens and closes its wings, as if to show the frog how to matter again.

Seventy years in the sun, and the rails on this old siding have begun to look weightless, cobwebs threaded through the grass. One day they may be lifted on the wind. Listen. Light footfalls. It's the mice with their pry bars of straw.

AUGUST

Black cows in deep shade under a mulberry tree, that part of its shadow that's swishing its tails. They have already eaten the cool, edible parts of the shade, the blue grass, the few violet leaves they could reach, and now they are waiting, their rumps bumped up together, tails slapping each other, gazing out through the flies at the blazing white pasture that goes on forever, that seems to be turning so slowly about them.

The trunks of the maples on Maple Street look as if they'd once been painted a pale, flat, bathroom green, but it's since been mostly rained away, leaving the surface cracked into mossy ribbons, and here and there a scuffed red knob has pushed out from a crack, and from that knob red twigs have sprouted all through the summer, springy and fresh. It's as if these trees, with their old limbs bony, broken, and swinging, have either forgotten their age or are merely pretending to still be alive. Or perhaps they've been inhabited by saplings who have whimsically put on battered uniforms and are trying to get a convincing creak in their voices whenever it's windy. Whatever the story, it's happening in tiny Dwight, Nebraska, where nearly everything else has been blown down, blown over, or blown away, and there's no Maple Street without a street of maples, so they're hanging on.

Someone is roofing a house in the distance, not a crew but a single do-it-your-selfer, and the pauses between the flat slaps of his nail gun tell us he's thinking it through, shingle by shingle, and praying for clear weather, the sun warm on the tarpaper under his knees.

I'd left my everyday walking shoes on the hardwood floor in the dining room when I went to bed, and when I picked up the left one, a tiny black spider sprinted out from under it and immediately slid under the right one. I put the left shoe on, tied it, set that foot down, and picked up the right one. The spider, again exposed, dashed in under my left foot, where there was apparently enough room between sole and heel. I put on the right shoe and then quickly stepped back, and the spider, suddenly out in the light, took a run at first one shoe and then the other, the former poet laureate hopping back, then apparently decided it was high time it looked for a more permanent shelter and zipped beneath the baseboard, where on its legs like spokes it wheeled around, stuck out its head and front legs, and stood ready for whatever came next.

In the tongue-and-groove ceiling, enameled white, two rusty holes where the heavy screw-eyes were, decades ago, and from which the porch swing hung on chains that made a crinkly, plunky music while we swung in pairs, scuffing the floor with our shoes, pushing in harmony to keep the swing flying, my grandparents, parents, my sister, and I, all of us taking turns swinging, forward and back, becoming stories, with time beneath our feet, enameled gray.

Somebody dumped this oily v8 engine, rolled it off a tailgate, tumbled it over and over, tipped it off a bank. The path is still fresh, but already a mouse has climbed the staircase of a manifold, tried the locked doors of the valves, and found just one ajar, with a round little room inside whose walls are curving mirrors. And now, as the red sun sets above the trickling creek, she moves her little bed in, straw by straw.

Like mine, the moon's eyelid is droopy. It too is old and has been around. We pass our time together without saying a word, like brothers scything weeds long after dark. His scythe has caught a little light, but mine has not. We still have work ahead, as long as we can see.

He walks like a windup toy, swinging his arms and rocking side to side on big shiny shoes. Someone has lovingly bathed and shaved him this summer morning, and fit his white legs into his slacks and his soft arms and bowling ball head into his golfer's shirt, and turned the key in his back and set him down and now he is ticktock stopping in front of the library and reaching down into the trash with the face of an angel, rose pink and the cool damp white of a bottle of milk, no wings but his lumpy, heaving shoulderblades as he bends like an obstetrician, extracting a handful of fries with ketchup, then turns to us smiling in triumph, and offers them dripping and alive.

There's a woman in Seward who is a talker, a talker, a talker. She was telling me that there's a group of men who meet for morning coffee in the deli section of the Pac 'N' Save, just off the produce section, and she's dying to be a part of their conversation but "it's a *guy* thing." She told me that sometimes when she's shopping she'll stand in the nearby produce section and contribute a comment or two from behind the banana display.

In late August, the level of summer has dropped, and one of the elm's little boats, faded green, with brown trim on its rails, turns at the end of a strand of cobweb far above the lawn. Whoever was in it has fallen away.

I saw an old man using a wooden chair for a walker, making his way up the street with the back of the chair in his hands as if pushing it up to a table. His mouth was loose and wet as he spoke to the past. Perhaps he was helping a woman into her place at a fancy dinner party forty or fifty years before, a big woman putting only a small part of her weight onto the chair as he carefully slipped it forward beneath her, the woman assisting by supporting herself on her legs and gripping the edge of the table, her buttocks resisting the chair seat, the young man embarrassed, apologetic, clumsily nudging the chair with his knee, the woman settling too far from the table, then seizing the seat in both plump hands and scooting forward, the wooden legs squealing and everyone turning to look at the woman's red face as she pinched her napkin out of her glass and shook it free, and staring at the young man's big white hands drawn forward, helpless, by that chair.

Here is a feather falling out of the sky, little more than a lock of white hair from the trailing edge of a blind old cloud, but as it falls, it becomes something else.

Can you feel how it spins out a kind of hysteria? There is something wrong with this pirouette, this daffy frenzy on the tip of a nerve; something about the way it reaches out this way and that, desperately snatching invisible somethings out of the air.

This cobra of plants, this weed, the common mulberry, lifts without a hiss from its basket of roots, stealthily eases itself through thorns and canes, rises into the light, and spits out a leaf. Cut it again and again and the root, a fistful of vipers, grows thick with resolve. For years it tries you again and again till your vigilance lapses. Then, in an instant, it lifts and slowly turns and spreads its scaly hood of leaves.

For the past few days, there's been a house four feet in the air at the edge of town, supported by beams on stacks of railroad ties. It's getting a new foundation.

One-story, hip-roofed, built in the era of Queen Victoria, it has squatted there watching the road into town for more than a century. Its windows, tall and ripply, have all week looked a little chagrined that its bottom was showing—a moist brown like a dead stump torn from the yard—and that it had been hefted against its will to a height that looked straight into a bedroom across the street. But today a crew came with a truck, and poured its new foundation, and to keep the concrete warm while drying fitted its waist with a heavy canvas skirt that sweeps the grass, all modesty.

In cap and dark blue uniform the pilot walks around the plane, a last pre-dawn, pre-flight inspection. Each of a hundred thousand rivets glints as he passes beneath, each step he takes is a meditation.

Flight is, in part, a complicated theorem, one that can't be chalked on any blackboard but the sky. You see the contrails up there, scratched against the blue. Part prayer, too, is flight. He understands the physics, yet bows his head and kneels before the heavy wheels, then touches one and backs away as if he'd left a votive candle guttering in time. He pauses a moment, alone and competent, within the great cathedral of the sky, beneath the lofty roof beam of the Milky Way.

At the town dump, at the oily foot of a great Mt. Horeb of trash, lie two old mattresses, side by side, gray tablets warped and bleached, upon which a single commandment is written: The vessel of thy body shall leak all the days of thy life.

This part of the darkness, a common skunk, strolls with a piece of white ribbon clenched in her teeth, the two ends trailing to either side, raising an eye-burning dust. Her eyes are fierce and black, with just enough room for two stars, and her stink can nudge open every loose door in the old chicken coop of your nose.

He gave up on his wife, my mechanic friend, gave up on trying hard to keep her home and halfway happy, leaving his work clothes on the side porch and scrubbing his hands with Orange Goop before he set one foot inside her kitchen, but it seemed that all she really wanted was music, gin rickeys, and other men by the score, sometimes just shiny-faced boys from the college, three or four to the car, who'd drop her at dawn and squeal away, leaving her drunk and stumbling, full of lies. So he turned the house over to her and bought a long low sofa for his shop and slept there for almost twenty years in greasy blue mechanic's overalls, carefully covering the cushions each night with the afternoon *Tribune*, after he'd read his bedtime story—yesterday's police report—to see if she'd gotten home all right.

The dented tin door to the diner's kitchen swings both ways, flaps open and shut like the valve on a steam vent, its hinges greased by sausage smoke, both link and patty, by eggs fried sunny-side up or over easy or scrambled with peppers and onions, by shouts and ancient arguments back with the black pots and pans.

The door's porthole is vacant, clouded over by numberless orders. It has suffered thousands of blows from the shoulders of women and girls, who bump their way through, one lunch hour at a time.

Old moon, he's planning a little vacation, just a few days away, but he's a fusser, that one, likes to take care of his things, so he's covered all his furniture with sheets of light—the trees, the supermarket parking lot, the streets of houses, even the back of a cat on a porch—just to keep the stardust off while he's away.

SEPTEMBER

One of our old neglected apple trees is so burdened with fruit this year that a limb has cracked, turned brown, and drapes limp-wristed, bejewelled with apples that ripen, day after day, on those lifeless fingers. This morning I noticed that hornets have come to set each garnet in a golden filigree.

Labor Day weekend, rainy and cool, and the second hatch of barn swallows are still in their nest under the eaves, three of them, downy and mewing, their beaks like buds just opening, while the rest of the swallows, an extended family of a dozen or more including the year's first hatch, wheel round and round this axis, crying, as if to unwind the invisible thread that holds them here, with winter coming.

Strung among withering leaves along a cantaloupe vine, a half dozen Japanese lanterns glow with a pale, parched light, their brown shades scorched to the point of sagging, while at the end of a fraying extension cord of squash vine one fat yellow lightbulb glows dimmer under the weeds.

I am afraid that the elf who comes in late November to unpack winter, tossing the tissue of snow, will never be able to undo the knots from this string of Christmas lights, these fat green cucumbers, burned out and black, cold to the touch.

I am tired of garden work, of trying to light my days with produce—the tapers of carrots, the fat votive candles of fresh tomatoes, the shuttered lanterns of eggplant—and so I turn away at last and leave them fading to darkness as the first leaves fall, like sparks, setting the fields afire.

All through the night a rain that is a woman with thin, cold hands, has been preparing this room in the corner of autumn, standing back for a look, then stepping forward again to adjust this or that. Her cold, wet fingertips touch everything once, then once again, but she is not pleased with the way things look: perhaps this yellow leaf needs to be turned just slightly and leaned against the brown.

Early in the morning, I push open the door to look outside and they drop like a hard rain out of the top of the frame where they've rested all night, a dozen or more moth millers—or is it miller moths?—fat as the tips of my fingers, tapping the porch floor with their dusty stupor. For a moment they lie still, some of them upside down or tipped on their sides against the dewy sill, their tiny black eyes bright but baffled, for they have slept so hard they've forgotten how to fly. They look a little like wood chips lying next to a stump where a man might have split kindling for his stove, but then, with a flutter, they right themselves, remembering that they have wings, and fly this way and that, into my hair, onto my nightshirt, into my face, as if I were made of a steady light and were irresistible, but I am not, just somebody at his open door, fussily brushing these chips away, struck chop by chop from dawn.

When she had finished letting down a cuff, or shortening a hem, or sewing a button back on a shirt, she'd pull the thread out tight, one lifting sweep and then another, as if she were conducting an orchestra of light and silence in that sunny room, then deftly knot off the music, clip the ends, and add them to a little nest of thread on the arm of her sewing chair. Not much of a nest, too loosely and carelessly woven, all orange and blue and white, and strong enough, it seems, to have held those hours I watched my mother at her work.

An old man in bib overalls and his wife in a housedress bring their blind daughter to lunch, a big woman of forty in slacks and a blouse, and those of us nearby are drawn within their love, dissolved within it, and, for a little while, the world is healed for us, a dozen ordinary customers, having the Wednesday special— pork roast, potato dumplings, kraut, and applesauce—served on styrofoam plates as autumn comes on, leading a few yellow cottonwood leaves up to the open door.

I like the looks of farm dumps, almost always filling a ditch in a pasture. What is no longer good for anything—from an Oldsmobile with a frozen crank to storm-tossed sheets of corrugated roofing—gets pushed off the edge, or over a hill, or into a cleft in a pasture, where time has been waiting in rain-gray coveralls with his cutting torch lit, its flame as red as a late September sumac leaf. For it's always September in these heaps of rust and brown, with field mice and rabbits setting up house for bad weather, claiming the driest tin cans or the dome of a fender.

High cirrus clouds like a toothy whistling and the woods in faded greens and browns like an old plaid shirt that the afternoon's thrown down, too warm to work in. And now, in a sweat-cooled undershirt of light, the breeze is picking what's left of the apples and sniffing them and tossing them away.

This town park is a place where people once played, and today it is all the more empty for that, with its swings on their chains looking like doorways thrown open to blowing leaves, and the merry-go-round like a bent tin top run down and tipped to one side. At last, after months, the teeter-totter has made up its mind as to which is the heavier end and has set that end down in the leaves. Overlooking the softball field, the bleachers—red, white, and blue—the enamel now blistered and split and the countersunk bolts rusty from dew, are warm to the touch from where the sun's big bottom sat for a while before the clouds blew in, and on the scuffed field, absence stretches to touch every base with the toe of its dusty shoe.

From a quarter mile off, my headlights awaken it, a red reflector, a half dollar–sized disk of foil and glass, a fierce eye in the night that came attached, like the gene for alertness, to the mailbox post my neighbors bought in the city where everything burns with watchfulness.

In the weeds by the road it snarls and bristles, waiting to snap at my tires as I pass, then drops back into the darkness, dark and disappointed.

The cows go where the ones ahead have gone, down the dusty bank to water, their front legs locked, their back legs bent to follow, each hoof scuffing more clay from the deepening cut of their path, slung bellies swollen with calves.

The cattle who came before, and the ones before those, stumbled and slid down this bank to drink, and drank of an earlier water, raising an older dust. The hooves of the young cows cut deeper and deeper as they follow the old into the present, leaving this path to the past.

The plumber carries a collapsible aluminum rod with a little round mirror hinged to one end, and with a flashlight can see around corners and up under things, discovering a stain on a joist or a stud that's been waiting to shine its own light back. For centuries, we let reflections lie, the mountain shining in a hoofprint brimmed with rain, and then somebody picked up something shiny and discovered that by turning it one could assemble all manner of glimpses into another world. And now the plumber does this without thinking, lying tense and heavy on the cellar floor, peering under the floor-length skirt of the broken water heater.

Some spider, done with this web, has left it for good, and a draft from the leaky cellar window has rolled it and pushed it aside, a furled sail of dirty gray on the long wooden dock of the sill, the mist of the season dried, the sailor gone who climbed up the side of the wind and rode there all day, doing his part of the world's long work by the light of a dusty pane.

Four in the morning, cold and still but for the buzz of my yard light as it talks to the one up the hill at my neighbor's. Mine says it feels the earth spinning it out to the end of its post, like a drop of light that might at any instant shake off into the stars, but my neighbor's says that's nonsense, the typical thing you can expect to hear from a poet's lamp: Nothing on earth can feel that centrifugal force. As for me, I know how light on their legs the fat mice are as they carry the dog food, nugget by nugget, feeling the warmth spin away from the earth, and how the trees are flushed at this time of the year with the effort of holding leaves. Oh, yes, there is a steady tug from the Milky Way, and I can feel my fingers lifting just a little away from these keys, not touching and then touching again, one tap and then another. So light I am, so light is my heart when I am up early, trying to write.

Walnuts, a whole universe of green planets under one tree, and my shadow falling upon them like the Unified Theory as I kneel to pick one up, feeling like God, feeling as if I had made them myself, forming them out of green mud, quite an accomplishment: Just think, one ounce of the future, straining to sprout from the dust of my hand.

Although for this old neighbor there is probably not much walking ahead, three extra pairs of shoes, still new and all alike, are shined and lined up next to the door, along with a long-handled shoe horn with a loop for his wrist. Beyond the door, his front lawn goes on day after day displaying in every drop of dew a possibility, but he is inside somewhere, behind drawn blinds, no longer casting a shadow, his knobby feet down there just out of reach, warm and dry in yesterday's stockings, not planning to carry him farther this morning than whatever needs to be done.

This new hammer handle now, the pleasure of fine-grained ash, light as a sparrow, and the pleasure of fitting it into the heavy, perched bird of the head and with a stand-by hammer driving the wedge, beating and beating it smooth, then the pleasure of swinging this bird-light, bird-heavy conjunction whose note is so clear that someone a quarter mile off knows just what's ringing.

On the bench in the barn where I park my chainsaw there's a small black pile of bat turds, dropped from the rafters each night while I am asleep, and each is exactly the size and shape of a capsule I take every morning, though mine is white, and so, according to some law of God or nature, it seems that the black pills all fall from the darkness, while the white, which taste slightly salty, all fall from the day.

Early this morning, the weatherman said we'd have five miles of visibility, and I thought I'd offer a little glimpse of what you might expect to find here, in a ten-mile circle of rolling fields closed in by yellow soybean harvest dust. Our hills are flesh-pink now from the bluestem's red stalks mixed in with bunch-grass ivory, and the leaves of the sumac, or buckbrush, are a scatter of apple peelings or, better, splashes of barn paint. Our little pond is a mirror with dirty dust-rag swirls of duckweed. Our flag snaps like a whip by the gravel road, where the rose hips redden under the mailbox and milkweed pods open their praying hands. In the distance, the dotty old grain trucks, dressed in pink and blue, come waddling and whimpering, peeing their pants, from behind barns, for their once-a-year trips to the co-op elevator, where the harvest—burnt red, peach-pink, and tangerine—has been augered into Egyptian pyramids in a grassy flat that was fifty years ago the railyard. And with our garden in weeds and overripe tomatoes, the windfall apples buzzing with yellow jackets, and the last lawn-mowing done and the lawn chairs stored in the loft of the barn, there is a little time to look around.

The chimney of this oil lamp is the silence surrounding a pipe organ that shimmers on top of the wick with no one to play it, or can that be a choir in golden robes, waiting to sing?

Whatever it is it glows with silence and patience. A person could sit here for hours, entranced by the light beneath the dark vaults in the church of the night, believing that grace, with a murmur of wings, will eventually come to the window.

Steady at forty-two degrees, the darkness has held its breath all night among the sleeping trees, carrying frost in its pockets but not taking it out, peering in through my window while waiting for just this moment, the lamp snapping on and suddenly revealing the fiery reds of my wife's big potted geranium that last night she carried in out of frost's reach just as the darkness stepped forward to snatch all the colors away.

OCTOBER

Each of these leaves had just one chance to feather the air with an arabesque of yellow or red, backlit and buoyant, just one chance to be held on the palm of the year, then briskly brushed away like an instant. Maybe two hundred leaves lie piled together under this empty maple, their jumpsuits weighing them down with color, the wind knocked out of them. Quickly it passed, but how well they did it, falling like that, just simply falling.

Over a barn door, a painted plank lintel, and on it a horseshoe, held by two nails and spattered with red from repainting beneath and around it, and above this, bunched on the top of the board and not much bigger than a walnut half, a gray-green tree frog, sleeping, up there in the warm October sun.

Oh, paper clip. Oh, you and me. For a time, we can hold a few disparate pieces together, a quarrelsome brother and sister, perhaps, or a mother and daughter-in-law, and manage to keep their edges perfectly aligned, their separateness fresh and intact. But sooner or later, our strength starts to fail, or we notice that the steady pressure has creased what we thought had been perfect, and left a rusty, indelible stain.

Just days from the first frost, on the pale gravel lane that leads out to the dawn, the year's last lightning bug glows like a pebble reflecting the moon. In the cracked rocks it lies weakened by cold, no longer flashing, a beacon that turned and turned over a warm summer sea sparkling with similar lights, but that this morning holds onto a steady glow, a pinhole in the curtain of time, letting in only a glimpse of eternity.

It seems that for this morning the burdens of the world have been set aside, for the people I meet on the path are carrying nothing but leaves, red and yellow, riding the toes of their shoes.

Repaired a broken step on the cellar stairs, though nobody goes down there but me, and I know where to set my weight, one foot at a time. But someone else may one day lift the door and step down, entering that silence creak by creak, and one small thing I fixed today may hold him up.

Oh, acorn, so you try a beret, but you still look, well, pretty ho-hum. You could sit there forever under your tree, hoping that someone might say hello, might lean down to tell you to have a nice day.

Wearing what's left of their uniforms, little more than a few mil-dewed tatters of khaki and brown, the sunflowers stand in rank and file in front of the cold gray barracks of a late autumn dawn, heads bowed, ready to accept whatever punishment is due them, fair or unfair, as the sun, a fat sergeant announced by a brass band of goose cries, arrives with the day, both hands out of sight behind his back.

Four slat-backed chairs pushed up around a back room table make a big bushel basket. Fill it up with smoky light and men in overalls and the hot rustle of pinochle cards and you have harvested enough for any rainy Friday.

By a country road, a slab of bedsprings plugging a gap in a fence, and a goat with yellow eyes behind it, peering through, the stinky ghost of someone's lust, finding a little nibble now and then.

My friend, how often have you dragged a set of bedsprings to the curb along with every memory it had to bear, and left it there, all sag and sentiment, hoping that someone will carry it off?

Just yesterday I watched a neighbor smooth his new yard with a garden tractor, dragging a storm of rusty bedsprings, two dozen singing cyclones clamped in layers, and when he finished not one clod was standing.

From the side of a tree to the feeder, then back to the side of the tree again and again and again, such is the nuthatch's work, wearing his little usher's uniform of blue and white, black capped, and, zip, here he comes, up the long cool aisle of a late afternoon, officious fellow, making a breeze as he swishes past, then zip, there he goes.

There was scarcely a hollow reed of wind at dawn, the bluestem stiff and reverent, not one fallen leaf that had budged an inch from its bed of frost, but on my walk I passed an old cottonwood trying to shush up its leaves, the biggest high school debate team ever assembled, waiting to crowd onto the yellow bus.

Oh, Halloween. A woman I once knew, dead twenty years, lived with her young, self-centered husband in a rented apartment on the upper floor of an ordinary, two-story, white frame house, and in their living room was a door, nailed shut, to the attic stair, with the doorknob removed, just part of the wall, painted the wall's cheap color, with their thrift store couch pushed up against it, and evenings when her husband had gone off on one of his self-important errands, and she was left alone to wait for him, reading by the light of their thrift store floor lamp, she'd hear soft footfalls coming down the attic steps to stand behind the door as if some spirit wanted in, or maybe wanted out. She said it didn't frighten her, but it was in some way comforting, holding its breath and waiting there behind her, teaching her the ways of patience with her husband gone.

That rusty water, drawn up by the cold pump, clank by clank, had so much iron in it that when we brought it flashing and dimpled to our lips it carried the odor of blood from the timeless darkness three hundred feet under our boots, and then we drank it, lustily.

This afternoon we have a cloudy sky right out of an Ernest Lawson painting: two blues, cerulean at the horizon and cobalt high above, with a half dozen grays in the heavy clouds that hold the blues behind them, randomly drawing apart to give us a glimpse of the universe, which is I think the cobalt, because the cerulean is closer and warm with the burnt red dust of soybeans being harvested. Outside this window where I write, two yellow butterflies are teaching two yellow ash leaves to fly, and they are starting to learn but are awkward and bump along on their stems like kites tugged over the grass. Though a friend gathered two bushels of windfalls for applesauce, the grass is cobbled under the tree and now and then Alice, our puppy, snatches an apple, hornets, worms, and all, and goes off at a gallop, tossing her head.

Such a wheezy old bellows my dog, Buddy, has become, no longer to snort hard into the eye-scalding flames of a badger's hole, or, from the top of a hill, to draw in a whole winter day with one breath.

And trick-or-treat. The littlest is afraid of her costume, a cat mask pressed over her nose and mouth like a sticky hand and, through the holes between the fingers, what used to be her older brother, mad and cackling, sacked in night and beribboned with phosphorescent bones. But her hand is nested in her father's hand as toward a stranger's door she stumbles, her shoes in the soft black bags of paws, long whiskers feeling through the night, and ahead of her, a life of many doors.

I have at last arrived at an age at which I can lean on a shovel while tending a fire of dry brush and see, as if on a brightly lit stage, all of the people I've known and loved, moving about among unfurled bolts of orange silk, blown by great fans from offstage left, one of those big crowd scenes in which the whole cast laughs and chatters together until one figure steps forward to speak in a clear voice, projecting his words from the edge of the stage, from the edge of the darkness where the rest of us wait, clutching unreadable programs, trying to hear what has happened.

NOVEMBER

November 1st, and a mile away, a hunter's shotgun raps once on the wet lid of the morning, and a yellow leaf comes loose and falls.

6:30 a.m., dark, still, and cold, and members of the marching band in down-filled jackets, stocking caps, and mittens, carrying instruments in cases black as dominos, or bellying great moony drums, or shouldering tubas, free hands pinching folders stuffed with music, trudge toward the stadium, not one among them talking to another, each walking sullen and apart, all sleepy, stumbly, slightly sour, each one a little part of something soon to be put together under the banks of lights already burning over a field as green as antifreeze, soon to be making their enormous, joyful, rumbling, brassy, honking, rattling, calamitous fanfare, rolling around and around the echoing bowl like a ball in roulette, a crash of sound right in the quiet intersection of night and morning, with both of the headlights smashed, nobody hurt, and sirens on the way.

In a stiff, cold rain, two geese glide over the chattering pond, elegant tourists, aloof and cosmopolitan, threading their way through a lobby, under the raindrop chandeliers. Just here for the day.

This fat silver star of a birthday balloon has been stopped in its ascent to the heavens by an ordinary ceiling, and now it floats there, belly up, dangling a length of string above the head of the woman whose birthday it is, who works at her desk long after hours, a big stack of years in the basket marked OUT, a few more waiting in the IN.

That faint glow as a picture tube cools in a darkening room is the same light coming from snowbanks at two in the morning, as if they were trying to hold on to yesterday's pleasures: the sitcom in which a dozen fat quail tried to fit under one small cedar, or the prime time game show in which an owl, perched on a fencepost, turned his head side to side, carefully choosing which shadow hid his fortune.

Even through curtains, the sun will assert itself enough to soften a candle, its warmth insistent as a kiss till the candle bends back. We all fall under the spell of the sun and are all at the end bent and consumed. See how a long row of fence posts leans over a deeply cut road as if they'd been pushed by the light.

When these cottonwoods were young they were all alike, set twenty feet apart along the road, the sisters mixed in with the brothers, each of them sprightly and yielding, scarcely casting a shadow, each leaf held out to catch the rain of sunlight, and all of the open air between them was every summer like a conversation, whispers of cottony foolishness lifting away on the breeze. But as they aged they drew closer together, shouldering in, their sagging branches searching for coins of sunlight in each other's pockets, some of their limbs already limp and swinging, a few bones dropped in the grass, and though today they still are all alive, each now looks nothing like the others, having its own long story but talking only to itself, leaning out over the old road drifted with leaves.

Again this morning, in a cold wind from the future, I walked all the way to the end of the long bridge of my life, having a look at its cables, its rods and rivets, its perforated metal flooring through which I could see whitecaps slamming the pylons. Then I turned and came back, inspecting it all from the other direction, fretting about every hex nut and bolt though they seem sound enough to hold things together. I ought to give the long bridge of my life a little rest, but every day it seems I'm walking from past to possibility and back to past with my brush and aluminum paint, hiding the rust, the deepening cracks, dabbing a shine here and there.

Not all of the raindrops are at rest on this high window looking down indifferently over the winter day (its glass rippled by age and touched with a pale violet light like the eyes of a very old woman). A few of the drops have begun to meander, hunching their silvery shoulders, clumsily jerking ahead, merging with others, assembling in columns (it being the traditional work of water to gather). But for the moment, most of the raindrops malinger. They stand together in little groups, shuffling their feet, white fists shoved into their jacket pockets, their muscular bodies fiercely shining.

This limberjack, this little wooden man dancing at the end of a stick is not me, of course, though his painted smile is much like mine. He is far better than I at entertaining, tappety-tap, tappety-tap, on the end of his plank, a charming fellow.

You may not even see me behind him, thrusting him into the light of your pleasure, making him dance, and at times, I too have lost myself in him, forgetting which is which, swinging my arms, waving hello and good-bye, the floor knocking hollowly under my feet.

The hunter waiting with his rifle ten feet up in a tree, knows that a deer, ever so cautious with every step, rarely looks up, and almost never sees its one last chance to run. Just now, in my nightshirt and slippers, walking the gravel lane to the road to get the Sunday paper, feeling a chill down my spine, I made a point of stopping to look at the stars.

The kind of *sad* in the word *sadiron* is a fierce, smoldering sorrow set squarely over the burner of anger. Your husband or wife runs off and the tears steam off your face. That sadness can press a sharp crease in your life that will never come out, though you wash in a hundred lovers.

I woke this morning thinking about a friend who died three years ago of cancer of the brain. She spent her last months reading books, packing her painfully swollen head with words that she would soon be taking into silence. From under her turban her blue eyes shone. I thought it peculiar that she would use up what little time she had left on learning, that she didn't want to be outside in the last of her seasons, an autumn and a winter, the cheerful yellow leaves, the immaculate snow, but I had forgotten—how could I have forgotten?—how much pleasure there is in being lost to time, alone with a book.

Four-thirty on a starry morning, and soon our *Journal Star* carrier will come roaring out of the east in his pickup, headlights like fists on the loose black reins of darkness, the road crunching under his tires, and slow down, stop, and drop the news in the dew-struck weeds under the mailbox. Without a pause he'll wheel around, the gravel flying, headlights sweeping the yard and house, and roar back east. Such resentment he must feel for us, here at the far end of the news, this house hidden in trees with just one window lit, where someone is up early writing.

A man-made satellite slowly pencils a line through one long passage in the lore of stars, but for those who know the constellation's stories, nothing can alter them.

Never a yellow like a weeping willow swaying in winter wind against a stand of dour gray elms and ash, and never a black quite like the arc you see scrawled on the side of an old tin shed where some young elm or ash all summer tossed its leafy top, but now stands naked, scarcely moving, held fast in front of what it did.

This morning, my wife and I shuffled through fallen leaves, those faded, wrinkled lists tossed aside by the trees once all of their tasks for the year have been checked off, and above us the early winter sky was clear and polished, empty but for a dust rag of cloud at one edge. The lake reflected all of this as if it were worth repeating, and it was, as were the two of us, had someone walking on the other side looked far across to see us, small and side by side, a couple married more than thirty years and walking through a world more beautiful to them with every passing season.

November, too, is nearly gone, nibbled away, bright leaf by leaf, by the mice of the wind, but here's a survivor, a pin oak open to the wind, not easily letting go of anything, red leaves like peeling paint against the cold gray planks and frosty nailheads of the dawn.

How quickly a fresh snow gives itself over, margin to margin, to the cuneiform writing of junco and mouse, out before sunrise, leaving brief notes for my dogs. And how time must enjoy it that no creature, hungry or frightened, can move even an inch without spoiling some surface, thus advancing the work of erasure.

DECEMBER

You've seen those telephone poles upon which hundreds of notices have been posted and then torn away: the lost, the found, the evenings' events, the faces of those who disappeared and then whose pictures vanished, too, leaving staples and scraps of paper. All of us think our lives unique, those pages that have been stapled up to tell the world of us, but this morning, all along the street, the old poles stand warming themselves, some leaning a little, holding one side to the sun, wrapped in our tattered life stories, every one alike, and coated with a frost of staples.

Our dreams go with us into the dark, but no one but the dreamer knew them anyway. Maybe it's not the soul that people at the bedside sometimes see, but all those dreams, with so much happiness forever sealed within them that they glow.

The holiday cocktail party begins at the door, where the trill of the doorbell flees from the vestibule and disappears into the crowd, leaving a vacuum of sound into which the small talk surges, foamy with greetings, a sea of hellos and how-are-you-doings that you can scarcely keep your head above, gulping for air as you paddle your way through the handshakes, showing your teeth. But ahead you can see, there in the kitchen, the raft of drinks, a-tinkle with glasses, and you grasp at its edge and with the others bark like a seal as the slow tide lifts you toward midnight, when with the deepest gratitude you know that somewhere upstairs your coat has just bobbed to the top of the pile on a bed and is drying its wings and waiting to lift you away.

·········

Always I feel as if there is a hand gently cupping the left side of my neck where they cut out the lymph nodes, as if someone I can't see were trying to make me feel better. It is probably Mother, come from the grave. But what I take to be her hand may be merely the way the nerves remember, as with her hand she held my neck to keep me from squirming away while she spit on the corner of her apron and wiped dirt from my face.

·········

With a sip of coffee I toast those sour-breathed ghosts, my mother and father, each with a favorite cup, their quiet winter Sunday morning talk; my bachelor uncle, Tubby, chair pulled up, his black Ford idling in the snowy drive, December pouring from his over-coat, mug hooked on his bone-white Methodist finger; my sister and I with bowls of Cheerios; all of us riding the steady little raft of a ring-stained, drop-leaf kitchen table that even then was drifting into the past with everything we ever were aboard, my uncle blowing a whistle of warnings across his cup, fears for a future he wouldn't reach but saw disaster in, the very days, in fact, we're living now.

·········

A pane of glass is a kind of compression of distance, enabling us to get up close to what we want but not permitting us to take it into our hands. We want it all, this life before us: the miniature Christmas village lit by a steady joy; the doll that in our arms would never grow old; the tiny train that, tooting, speeds away and always returns. Yet our lives are not beyond this breath there on the chilly glass, but of that breath, and in this life the hands in our mittens are never really empty. It is all around us, free, this wonderful life: clear jingle of tire chains, the laughter of ice that breaks under our boots. Each hour's a gift to those who take it up.

In those old movies, to show us the passage of days, pages blew from a calendar, number by number, somersaulting off to the left as if that was the direction in which the past had flown. The directors wanted to get on with the action; they didn't turn their lenses to where those days had drifted up, in rain, against a chain-link fence at the end of an alley. There, a few of us, down on damp knees, sort through the clutter, arranging the past despite the missing pages, carefully piecing the torn days together. At times, unable to sleep, we find ourselves working all night by thin light from the stars.

A skillful man can snatch a tablecloth from under a full setting of dishes and leave it just as it stood, the goblets whining but still on their stems. Just so the winter trees in these backyards have felt spring, summer, and autumn snatched from beneath them, but still they stand, light whispering through. I too have felt it, walking an alley where I played as a child, seeing the trees I climbed grown tall and creaky, the years swept from under my feet along with every smoking cinder my father shoveled from our furnace. And where I stood a while and listened, I felt a glassy leaflessness.

I talked to a man in a clinic waiting room who as I watched him had, first, tinkered with a jigsaw puzzle and then had played a game of solitaire on a computer. A big man, maybe seventy, with soft, Charles Laughton lips. He told me his wife was there for chemo after lung cancer surgery. She had been the wife of his best friend, now dead, and he said she'd smoked until just three years ago. He was born on a farm and has taught vocational agriculture, farmed, and done this and that to get by. He had some stories about hard times in the '30s, and told me one about a paternal uncle who was a traveling salesman and drove all over Kansas with a lister, a kind of moldboard plow, on a flatbed trailer behind a Model A. He said that one spring when the ag business looked promising the uncle took orders for all of his inventory and sent home a telegram. When you sent a telegram you paid by the word, and times were hard. The telegram read:

SOLD OUT, L. W.

I like the idea of there being times when even words cost so much you used them sparingly. I have known a lot of old men and women who talked as if they were paying Western Union by the word.

Receiving the news of a death, I stepped to the front of my sadness and worry, and shook out the rag rug of the past, made it snap in the morning light, and memories glittered like stars, with here and there a speck of color or a wisp of hair though it was only common dust to anyone but me.

I knew a shy old man whose long hands swung from the cuffs of his shirts like these ice-coated branches sweeping the shadowy yard in the light from the kitchen window. He was good with machines, but when his fingers were empty of work he had no place to hide them. They never quite fit in his pockets. For more than eighty winters, he sat just inside the loose door to the world, watching his wife in her kitchen. His fingers brushed a table there, feeling for something that ought to be tightened. By the light of the kitchen window tonight, I see him out there on the threshold showing his hands to my aunt, how clean he's got them, scrubbing them over and over.

You have been gone for fifty years, but when washed, your good china looks new, the way it must have looked when you unpacked it. I have it set out on our dining room table ready for Christmas, and the light from the lamp by which I write this to you—a brief note to the past—glints on the gold trim, one glint for each plate and cup and saucer as if the light were touching it where once you touched it, long ago, unwrapping it when it was new.

Easing myself through a tiny vent in my forgetfulness, I discover draped over my outstretched fingers a rustling chain of red and green construction paper, just now finished, loopy link by link, LePage's paste still soapy on the air and Mother's sewing scissors sticky on the carpet more than sixty years ago, and others of the family near me—Sister, is that you?—And now I see the tree with its blown-glass birds with comet tails, the bobbing balls and tops and spindles, a string of lights set into bent tin stars and fragrant branches reaching out to take this flimsy garland from my hands.

I once read of a climber who, while clinging to the face of a cliff thousands of feet above an alpine valley, said he could feel the earth turn under his hands. And I have read that a person with patience could move an aircraft carrier tied at a dock by leaning long enough against its side to get it started, knowing that once it began to move there'd be no bringing it back, and it came to me that the earth behaves like that, moving steadily out into time under the common pressure of billions of hands.

No stopping it now.

What does the earth's shadow look like flying through space? A jellyfish, perhaps, swimming at the speed of light with filaments streaming behind. At sunrise or sunset, if you stand on a hilltop, with your arms spread out and your fingers fluttering like feathers, your shadow can ride at the top of that enormous, flying darkness, racing forever into the stars.

ACKNOWLEDGMENTS

"One of my mother's Moser uncles . . ." published as "Horticulture" in *Shenandoah*.

"And another of my friends . . ." published as "A Death" in *Able Muse*.

"The passing years . . ." published as "Old Sidewalk" in *Narrative*.

"Strung among withering leaves . . ." published as "Late Summer Garden" in *Solo*.

"Early in the morning . . ." published as "A Letter in June" in *Eleventh Muse*.

"When she had finished . . ." published as "The Nest of Thread" in *Spirituality and Health*.

"This town park . . ." published as "Town Park, Late Autumn" in *Ibbetson Street*.

"The chimney of this oil lamp . . ." published as "Oil Lamp" in *Solo*.